gr 4-6

ULTIMATE CARS

Ferrari

Rob Scott Colson

PowerKiDS
press.

New York

Published in 2011 by The Rosen Publishing Group Inc.
29 East 21st Street, New York, NY 10010

Copyright © 2011 Wayland/
The Rosen Publishing Group, Inc.

First Edition

Editor: Camilla Lloyd
Produced by Tall Tree Ltd
Editor, Tall Tree: Emma Marriott
Designer: Jonathan Vipond

Library of Congress Cataloging-in-Publication Data

Colson, Rob Scott.
  Ferrari / by Rob Scott Colson. -- 1st ed.
      p. cm. -- (Ultimate cars)
  Includes bibliographical references and index.
  ISBN 978-1-61532-854-3 (library binding)
  ISBN 978-1-61532-627-3 (paperback)
  ISBN 978-1-61532-628-0 (6-pack)
  1. Ferrari automobile--Juvenile literature. I. Title.
  TL215.F47C653 2011
  629.222'2--dc22

                                    2009045412

Photographs
Cover Shell, 1 Mtoome/Dreamstime.com, 2 Shell, 4 fastcars/
Alamy, 5t Gabigarcia/Dreamstime.com, 5b TiConUno
s.r.l./Alamy, 6 Transtock Inc./Alamy, 7 Shell, 8–9 Shell,
8t Shell, 9 Mtoome/Dreamstime.com, 11b culture-
images/MPI/Hans Dieter Seufert, 12 Thomas
doerfer/GNU, 14 Mikaël Restoux/GNU, 15t
Transtock Inc. / Alamy, 15b Sfoskett/GNU,
16 Tom Wood / Alamy, 17t Dave Lethbridge/
GNU, 17b David Monniaux/GNU, 18 Shell,
19t Klemantaski Collection/Getty Images, 19b
Shell, 20–21 Shell, 21 Shell, 24 Shell

Manufactured in China

CPSIA Compliance Information: Batch #WAS0102PK: For Further Information
contact Rosen Publishing, New York, New York at 1-800-237-9932

Contents

Ferrari

Ferraris are the most famous sports cars in the world. Since their first road car, the 125 S, left the factory in 1947, the Italian company have made a string of models for the road and the racetrack.

All Ferraris are designed for maximum performance, which means that they can accelerate (increase speed) quickly and reach very fast top speeds.

A Ferrari Enzo being put through its paces on the test track in 2002. A road-legal car, the Enzo has a top speed of 217 mph (350 kph).

Michael Schumacher in action in 2005. The German driver won the Formula 1 Drivers' Championship with Ferrari five years in a row, from 2000–2004.

Team Ferrari

The racing wing of the company is known as Scuderia Ferrari (Team Ferrari). It was founded in 1929 by a young racing driver named Enzo Ferrari, who ran a team of drivers for the Alfa Romeo car company. Ferrari started making their own racing cars after World War II. They have competed in motor racing's ultimate challenge, Formula 1, ever since it began in 1950, and a Ferrari driver has been Champion Driver a record 15 times.

Enzo Ferrari

Enzo Ferrari (1898–1988) took huge pride in the speed of his cars and the daring of his drivers. To reflect that spirit, his racing team adopted the famous "Prancing Horse" logo, which had been the good luck symbol of World War I fighter pilot, Francesco Baracca. Ferrari's passion for his cars rubbed off on everyone who worked for him. In 2007, Ferrari was voted the best workplace in Europe. After all, the very best cars need the very best workers to make them.

Enzo Ferrari at the wheel of an Alfa Romeo in a race in 1923.

612 Scaglietti

The 612 Scaglietti is a grand tourer, which means that it is a high-performance sports car designed for driving long distances in comfort.

The huge 5.7 liter engine produces 540 brake horsepower (the unit used to measure an engine's power). That's five times more powerful than the cars most people drive. There is room for all the family inside the 612 Scaglietti, but they had all better be strapped in!

Big but Light

The 612 Scaglietti only has two doors, but it is a big car with room for four adults to sit in comfort. Big cars are heavy, and weight slows cars down. The 612 Scaglietti's chassis—the framework of metal bars that acts as its skeleton—and the body panels welded onto it are both made entirely of lightweight aluminum, rather than the heavier steel. This reduces the car's weight by 40 percent, allowing it to reach speeds of over 195 mph (300 kph) despite its size.

STATS AND FACTS

YEARS OF PRODUCTION **2004–present**
ENGINE SIZE **5.7 liter**
NUMBER OF CYLINDERS **12**
TRANSMISSION **Manual (Stick shift)**
GEARBOX **6-speed**
0–62 MPH (0–100 KPH) **4.2 seconds**
TOP SPEED **195 mph (315 kph)**
WEIGHT **4,054 lb. (1,839 kg)**
CO_2 EMISSIONS (G/KM) **475**
FUEL ECONOMY **13.6 mpg (20.7 L/100 km)**

The sunroof becomes darker on a bright day.

Amazing Design

Everything in this grand tourer is designed to provide luxury to the long-distance driver. The glass panel in the roof is photochromic. This means that it becomes darker in bright sunlight, just like "Reactolite" sunglasses. The panel changes automatically to let in between 5 percent and 95 percent of the light, so that it is never too bright or too dark inside the car.

The 612 Scaglietti is designed to look very similar to a special one-of-a-kind Ferrari custom-built for actress Ingrid Bergman in 1954.

California

Ferrari's latest model is every bit as quick as their other cars, but has a softer, more curvy shape, and the company hope women will want to drive it.

High-performance cars are often bad for the environment because they burn a lot of fuel and emit (give off) more carbon dioxide, a gas that is contributing to global warming. With carbon dioxide emissions at the same level as much slower cars, the California is less of a guilty pleasure than other Ferraris.

Double Clutch

The California has seven different gears. To change gear, cars have to disconnect the engine from the wheels using the clutch, which usually causes a temporary loss of power. The California has two clutches—one for odd-numbered gears and another for even-numbered ones. The driver can change gear without losing power by moving smoothly from one clutch to the other.

The driver changes gear using shifts on the steering wheel.

Amazing Design

The California is a convertible, which means that its roof can retract (fold back) on sunny days. It retracts neatly into the trunk at the touch of a button in just 14 seconds. Many convertibles have soft roofs, which makes them light, but can mean that they are not comfortable in cold weather. The California's hard roof provides more protection in bad weather, but weighs 11 lb. (5 kg) less than a soft roof, so the driver gets the best of both worlds. There is not much room for a picnic basket with the roof in the trunk, though!

The back opens up automatically as the roof retracts.

Currently, just 15 percent of Ferrari drivers are women. The company hope the California's softer shape and lower emissions will attract more women.

STATS AND FACTS

YEARS OF PRODUCTION **2009–present**
ENGINE SIZE **4.3 liter**
NUMBER OF CYLINDERS **8**
TRANSMISSION **Dual-clutch manual**
GEARBOX **7-speed**
0–62 MPH (0–100 KPH) **4 seconds**
TOP SPEED **limited to 193 mph (310 kph)**
WEIGHT **3,593 lb. (1,630 kg)**
CO_2 EMISSIONS (G/KM) **305**
FUEL ECONOMY **21.6 mpg (13 L/100 km)**

Testarossa

The Ferrari Testarossa was a sports car that became a symbol of style in the 1980s when it appeared in the hit TV show, *Miami Vice*.

Its name is Italian for "red head" and refers to the color of the cam covers that fit on top of the engine. It is hard to find a Testarossa that isn't painted red all over, however, and it is the color that is most associated with Ferrari cars.

The 512 TR

In 1991, Ferrari redesigned the Testarossa, giving it a more powerful engine. The new car was called the 512 TR, and could accelerate from 0–62 mph (0–100 kph) in 4.8 seconds—half a second faster than the Testarossa. The 512 TR's distinctive sharp "wedge" shape is very aerodynamic, which means that it cuts a path through the air as it travels forward. The Stats and Facts here are for the 512 TR.

The Testarossa's engine is in the middle of the car to balance its weight evenly and make it easier to control at high speed.

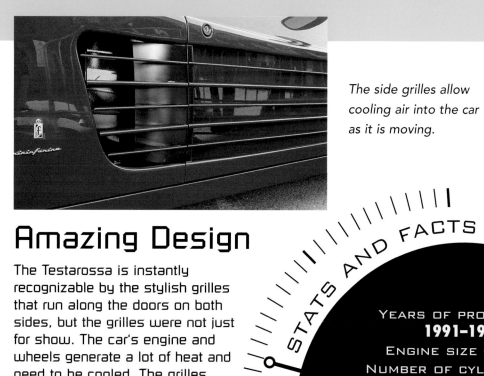

The side grilles allow cooling air into the car as it is moving.

Amazing Design

The Testarossa is instantly recognizable by the stylish grilles that run along the doors on both sides, but the grilles were not just for show. The car's engine and wheels generate a lot of heat and need to be cooled. The grilles allow air into the car to cool it down. Taking air into the engine can slow it down by increasing the car's air resistance. The side grilles allow air that is not taken in to flow smoothly around the car, minimizing air resistance.

STATS AND FACTS

YEARS OF PRODUCTION **1991–1994**
ENGINE SIZE **4.9 liter**
NUMBER OF CYLINDERS **12**
TRANSMISSION **Manual (Stick shift)**
GEARBOX **5-speed**
0–62 MPH (0–100 KPH) **4.8 seconds**
TOP SPEED **195 mph (314 kph)**
WEIGHT **3,243 lb. (1,471 kg)**
CO_2 EMISSIONS (G/KM) **not available**
FUEL ECONOMY **14.4 mpg (19.6 L/100 km)**

The Testarossa is a coupé, which means that its roof cannot be removed.

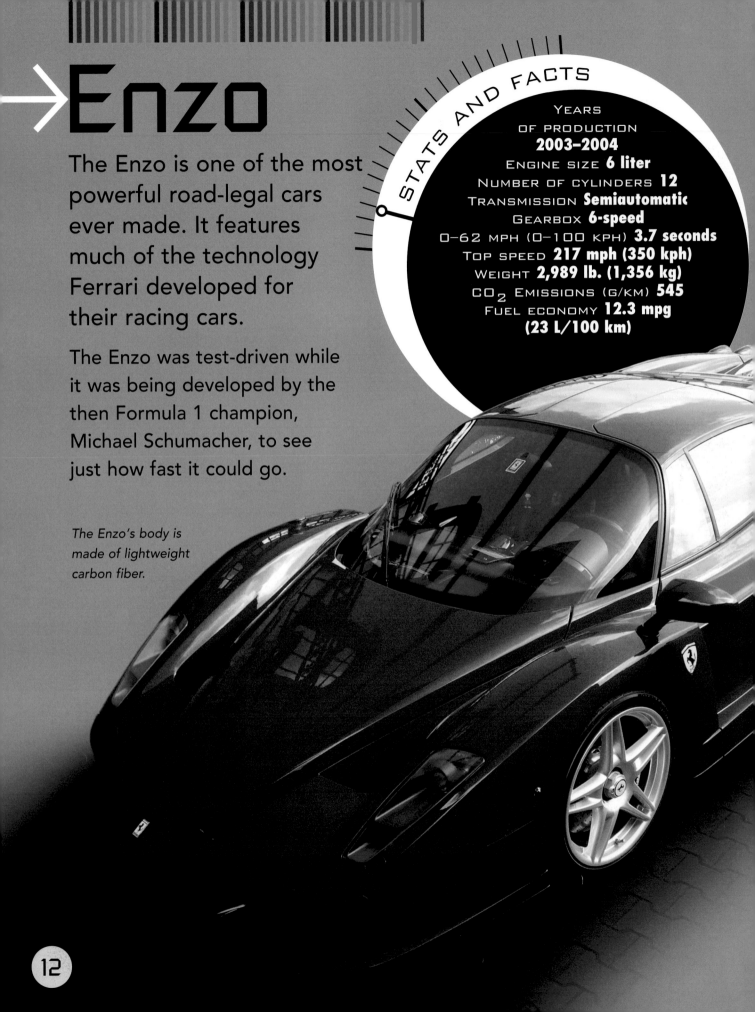

Enzo

The Enzo is one of the most powerful road-legal cars ever made. It features much of the technology Ferrari developed for their racing cars.

The Enzo was test-driven while it was being developed by the then Formula 1 champion, Michael Schumacher, to see just how fast it could go.

The Enzo's body is made of lightweight carbon fiber.

STATS AND FACTS

YEARS OF PRODUCTION
2003–2004
ENGINE SIZE **6 liter**
NUMBER OF CYLINDERS **12**
TRANSMISSION **Semiautomatic**
GEARBOX **6-speed**
0–62 MPH (0–100 KPH) **3.7 seconds**
TOP SPEED **217 mph (350 kph)**
WEIGHT **2,989 lb. (1,356 kg)**
CO_2 EMISSIONS (G/KM) **545**
FUEL ECONOMY **12.3 mpg (23 L/100 km)**

The engine produces its maximum power of 660 bhp (brake horsepower) when it is working at 7,800 rpm (revolutions per minute).

Amazing Design

The Enzo's engine is connected directly to the gearbox using a system known as sequential shift transmission. This technology was developed for Formula 1. It allows the driver to change gear without disconnecting the engine from the wheels, which loses power. The Enzo can change gear in an incredible 150 thousandths of a second—literally the blink of an eye—which means that it accelerates very smoothly.

Scissor Doors

Not only is the Enzo one of the fastest road cars ever made, it is also one of the widest, at over 6.5 feet (2 m) across. That's about 16 inches (40 cm) wider than an ordinary car. To allow the driver and passenger in and out on narrow city streets, the doors swing upward from a hinge at the front. These are known as "scissor doors."

Scissor doors are also known as "beetle-wing doors" as they open like the wings of an insect.

250 GTO

The 250 GTO was a sports car built to compete in endurance races where cars must drive as far as they can in a set time limit.

It was an instant success, winning the World Manufacturers' Championship in all three years of its production. Its design was kept basic to keep weight to a minimum. It did not have a speedometer, so drivers would guess how fast they were going by the gear they were in and the sound of the engine.

STATS AND FACTS

Years of production **1962–1964**
Engine size **3 liter**
Number of cylinders **12**
Transmission **Manual (Stick shift)**
Gearbox **5-speed**
0–62 mph (0–100 kph) **5.8 seconds**
Top speed **limited to 174 mph (280 kph)**
Weight **2,425 lb. (1,100 kg)**
CO_2 Emissions (g/km) **Not available**
Fuel economy **Not available**

GT Class

Although the 250 GTO was made to race on the track, it competed in a class of racing known as GT (short for *Gran Turismo*, Italian for "grand tourer"). Cars in the GT class had to be road-legal and, officially at least, 100 cars had to be sold to the public. Ferrari were allowed to compete after promising to build the minimum number of cars, but in the end, only 36 were ever made for sale. They are now extremely rare and worth a great deal of money. In 2008, a 250 GTO sold at auction for a record $23.5 million. Start saving!

The engine had 12 cylinders set in a "V" shape.

Amazing Design

The GTO's engine is at the front of the car. Racing cars now all have their engines behind the driver, since this gives the car a better weight distribution and makes it easier to handle. All engines need to be kept well lubricated with oil. The GTO used "dry sump" lubrication, which means that a store of oil was kept below the engine. This helped to lower the car's center of gravity, keeping it firmly on the track at high speeds.

Dino

Dino was the name of a series of mid-engined sports cars produced by Ferrari between 1968 and 1976. The Dino was the first Ferrari to be made in relatively large numbers, with 4,000 produced in the first five years of production.

This move toward mass production was a direct result of racing regulations. In order to compete in Formula 2 series racing, at least 500 road cars had to be made using the same engine.

A 206 Dino from 1968. The Stats and Facts, left, are for this model.

STATS AND FACTS

Years of production **1968–1969**
Engine size **2 liter**
Number of cylinders **6**
Transmission **Manual (Stick shift)**
Gearbox **5-speed**
0–62 mph (0–100 kph) **7.5 seconds**
Top speed **146 mph (235 kph)**
Weight **2,513 lb. (1,140 kg)**
CO_2 Emissions (g/km) **Not available**
Fuel economy **Not available**

The lights lie flat to the hood when not in use, and pop up electrically when needed.

1970s Wedge

Early Dinos had the curvy bodywork typical of 1960s sports cars. Later models, such as the Dino 308 GT4, above, first made in 1973, were wedge-shaped. Like the Enzo that came after it, this wedge shape may not have looked as good, but it made the cars more aerodynamic. To make the Dino as sleek as possible, it was fitted with pop-up lights that sat hidden when not in use in order not to cause air resistance.

The interior of the Dino was basic, but it still had luxurious leather seats.

Amazing Design

The cockpit of the Dino range was more basic than those of more expensive Ferrari models. The Ferrari factory was not big enough to make large numbers of cars, so to meet their production target, they teamed up with the mass car producer, Fiat. The result was a less expensive, although still stylish, model to compete with cheaper rival sports cars such as the Porsche 911.

Formula 1

Scuderia Ferrari have competed in every season of Formula 1, winning the Constructors' Championship (the total points score of the teams' two drivers) a record 16 times.

Ferrari spend tens of millions of dollars each year developing a new car for the Formula 1 season. The most successful team ever, they have a large and passionate band of Italian fans known as the *tifosi*, who all dress in Ferrari T-shirts at the Italian Grand Prix, filling the grandstands with a sea of red.

Kimi Raikkonen won the driver's championship in a Ferrari in 2007.

Alberto Ascari on his way to victory at the 1952 British Grand Prix at Silverstone.

STATS AND FACTS

YEARS OF PRODUCTION **1952–1953**
ENGINE SIZE **2 liter**
NUMBER OF CYLINDERS **4**
TRANSMISSION **Manual (Stick shift)**
GEARBOX **4-speed**
0–62 MPH (0–100 KPH) **9 seconds**
TOP SPEED **165 mph (265 kph)**
WEIGHT **1,235 lb. (560 kg)**
CO_2 EMISSIONS (G/KM) **Not available**
FUEL ECONOMY **Not available**

Success

The first Ferrari driver to win the Formula 1 drivers' championship was Italian Alberto Ascari in 1952. He dominated the season, winning six out of the eight races. Motor racing in those days was very dangerous, and crashes were often fatal. The car Ascari drove, the Tipo 500, had very few safety features, and he was killed in a crash during a race in 1955.

To be successful in Formula 1, a driver needs a skilled team behind him. During a race, cars make one or more "pit stops" to change tires and take on more fuel. A team of about 20 highly trained mechanics performs the whole operation in under 10 seconds. A bad pit stop could lose the driver the race.

Three mechanics are needed to change each wheel.

Fuel is pumped into the engine quickly using high pressure.

Formula 1 Car

Formula 1 teams must follow strict rules when building their cars.

The car must be a minimum weight and the engine must be no larger than 2.4 liters. Devices for making the engines more powerful, such as turbochargers, are not allowed. The rules change regularly, so each team must build a new car every year. This is the car Ferrari built for the 2008 season.

Air intake passes air over the engine to keep it cool.

rear wing

The eight-cylinder engine sits behind the driver. Placing the engine and driver around the middle of the car makes sure that weight is evenly distributed between front and back.

The tires have a minimum of four grooves in them. This rule was introduced to slow the cars down. "Slick" tires with no grooves were allowed back for the 2009 season.

The main body of the car is made of light but very strong carbon fiber.

20

A Car with Wings

The car's wings disrupt the flow of air over the car, creating downforce that keeps it safely on the track. Downforce is important when the car is cornering, as side forces could make the driver lose control. Downforce reduces top speed on the straight, but increases speed around corners.

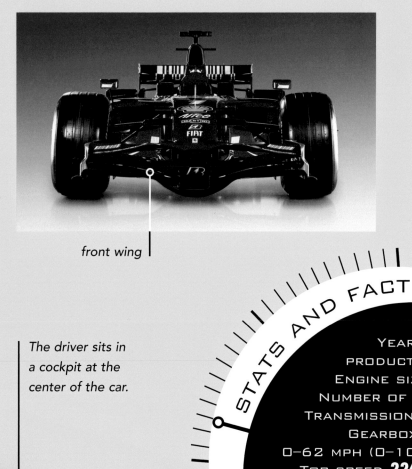

front wing

The driver sits in a cockpit at the center of the car.

STATS AND FACTS

YEARS OF PRODUCTION **2008**
ENGINE SIZE **2.4 liter**
NUMBER OF CYLINDERS **8**
TRANSMISSION **Semiautomatic**
GEARBOX **7-speed**
0–62 MPH (0–100 KPH) **2 seconds**
TOP SPEED **224 mph (360 kph)**
WEIGHT **1,334 lb. (605 kg)**
CO_2 EMISSIONS (G/KM)
Approx. 230 metric tons per season
FUEL ECONOMY **2.8 mpg**
(100 L/100 km)

front wing

Glossary

accelerate
To increase speed.

air resistance
The force of the air against the car as it moves. The shape of a car is designed to keep air resistance to a minimum by allowing the air to pass smoothly around it.

brake horsepower (bhp)
Unit of measurement for an engine's power.

carbon fiber
A lightweight modern material often used instead of metal.

center of gravity
The point around which a car is balanced. If its center of gravity is low and half way along the car, it is said to be well-balanced.

chassis
The frame or skeleton of the car to which the body and the engine are attached.

clutch
A means of disconnecting the engine from the wheels in order to change gear.

cylinder
A chamber in an engine inside which pistons pump up and down, producing the engine's power.

fuel economy
The rate at which a car uses fuel. It is measured in miles per gallon (mpg) or liters per 100 kilometers (L/100 km).

gear
A system of cogs that control the transfer of power from the engine to the wheels. Low gears are used for for acceleration or driving uphill. High gears are used for driving at faster speeds.

handling
The ease with which a driver can control the car using the steering wheel.

hood
A hinged panel that covers the engine at the front of a car.

logo
A distinctive design that identifies the company that made a product.

mph
Short for miles per hour, a measurement of speed. Kilometers per hour is "kph."

performance
A measurement of a car's power and handling. A car that accelerates quickly and has a high top speed is said to be a high-performance car.

transmission
The way in which a car transfers power from the engine to the wheels via a gearbox that allows the driver to change gear.

turbocharger
A device that makes an engine more powerful by recycling exhaust gases.

Models at a Glance

Model	Years Made	Numbers Built	Did You Know?
Tipo 500	1952	1	Alberto Ascari won nine races in a row in the Tipo 500. The car was only ever beaten in one Grand Prix.
250 GTO	1962–64	36	After its first season racing, three other teams tried to get the GTO disqualified. They failed.
Dino 246	1969–73	2,487 (just the 246 GT model)	The Ferrari Dino was named after Enzo Ferrari's son, Alfredo (Dino for short), who died in 1956 age 24.
Testarossa	1984–96	10,000	Only one convertible Testarossa, known as the Testarossa Spider, was ever built.
Enzo	2003–04	401	The last Enzo ever to be built was sold at auction in aid of charity for $1.4 million.
612 Scaglietti	2004–present	N/A	Customers are invited to the factory to choose the interior details they would like with Ferrari's designers.
California	2009–present	Ferrari plan to build 5,000 by 2011	The California's body is made from lightweight aluminum, which makes it more fuel efficient.
Formula 1 car	A new model is built each year	Two cars are entered in each race	The 2009 car looks very different from the 2008 model. It has a low front wing and a narrow rear wing.

Further Reading

Blazers: Ferrari
by Lisa Bullard
(Capstone Press, 2007)

Ferrari
by Rainer W Schlegelmilch
(H F Ullmann, 2008)

Ferrari: A Complete Guide to all Models
by Leonardo Acerbi
(Motorbooks, 2006)

Web Sites

Due to the changing nature of Internet links, PowerKids Press has developed an online list of Web sites related to the subject of this book. This site is updated regularly. Please use this link to access this list:
http://www.powerkidslinks.com/uc/ferrari

Index